Stuck on a Loop

Can't make a mistake.

Paula Nagel

Illustrated by Gary Bainbridge

Routledge
Taylor & Francis Group

LONDON AND NEW YORK

First published 2017
by Routledge
2 Park Square, Milton Park, Abingdon, Oxon OX14 4RN

and by Routledge
711 Third Avenue, New York, NY 10017

Routledge is an imprint of the Taylor & Francis Group, an informa business

British Library Cataloguing-in-Publication Data
A catalogue record for this book is available from the British Library

Library of Congress Cataloging-in-Publication Data
A catalog record for this book has been requested.

ISBN: 978 1 90930 177 1 (pbk)
ISBN: 978 1 31517 492 1 (ebk)

Typeset in Univers Light Condensed
by Moo Creative (Luton)

Visit the eResources: www.routledge.com/9781909301771

Printed and bound by CPI Group (UK) Ltd, Croydon, CR0 4YY

3

Gemma always takes such good care of her school things...
If you tap your pencil three times, you won't make any mistakes.
So organised!
tap
tap
tap

Gemma
Spellings
1. programme ✓
2. average ✓
3. curiosity ✓
4. vehicle ✓
5. category ✓
6. desperate ✓
7. leisure ✓
8. recognise ✓
9. privilege ✓
10. physical ✓
10/10
Well done Gemma!

Panel 1: It's normal to feel a bit worried about tests, but try not to worry too much.

Panel 2: Tests are a way of practising what you already know and finding out what you still need to know.

Panel 3: I know I'll make a mistake.
one...
two...
three.

Panel 4: Don't worry about making a mistake...

But if we use all of our brain space to worry, we'll have nothing left for thinking about the spellings themselves.
One...
Can't make a mistake.
two...
If I see three white vans...
three.

One...
two...
three...
Can't make a mistake.
Tap...
tap...
tap...
Tap...
tap...
tap...
Got to see another van.
Just one more.
One...
two...
three...

P You may photocopy this page for instructional use only. © 2017, *Stuck on a Loop*, Paula Nagel & Gary Bainbridge, Routledge.

Thoughts? what kind of thoughts?
I know it sounds really silly...
But thoughts that tell you to do things so that everything will be OK.
Bossy thoughts?
I suppose so.

Thoughts like...

"You must hold your breath when you go past the dentist's surgery or else you'll get a bad tooth"?

Or...

"You have to see three vans and then you'll do well in the test."

'Stuck on a Loop' Workbook 4

Let's talk about ...
when thoughts get stuck

Here's Gemma to tell you what she learned about stuck, unhelpful thoughts.

We all have thoughts running through our minds.

Thoughts can be helpful and let us work things out and solve problems.

I'm a bit worried about starting my new class on Monday. I think I'll call my friends to see if they want to meet over the weekend. Maybe they're feeling the same way too ...

Tom hasn't replied to my text yet. That's not like him. I wonder if I should call him to see if he's OK, or send another text ...

But, sometimes, thoughts can be unhelpful.

Unhelpful thoughts might seem stuck.

In my story, my thoughts were unhelpful because they became stuck and went round and round on a loop in my mind.

Have you ever had a tune, a song or a jingle stuck in your mind? It can feel as if it will never go away ... and the more you try to forget it, the more it sticks.

Stuck thoughts can be a bit like this. Stuck thoughts leave no room for any other thoughts.

Thoughts can get stuck when we worry about things, or feel stressed or under pressure.

Sometimes, thoughts can become stuck when we feel tired or physically unwell.

Look back at my story. When did my stuck thoughts happen? Write or draw about them on the hamster wheel below.

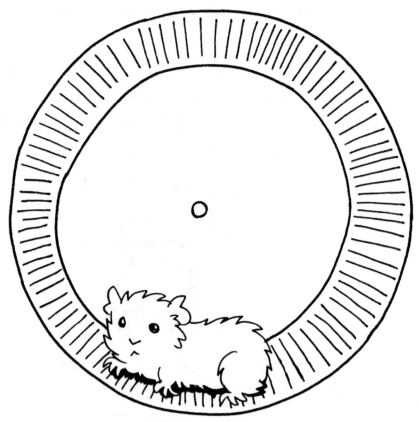

My thoughts became stuck when I worried about the tests. I was worried about making a mistake.

Remember: a little bit of worry can be a good thing, and help us prepare for things like tests and exams, by helping us to feel alert, ready to face the challenge, and do our best.

But when worry grows big, and becomes stuck, then it can be unhelpful. We can get stuck in the habit of worrying.

Sometimes big, stuck thoughts tell us to do things we don't really want to do.

These thoughts might be bossy and tell us we need to do something to stay safe or to bring good luck.

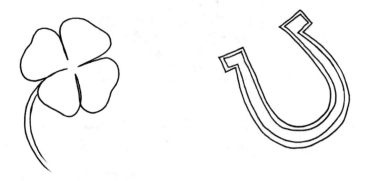

When we do what the stuck, bossy thought says, we might feel better for a little while. It doesn't last though ... the thoughts can get stronger, take over and become a habit.

46

I worried about spelling tests and
getting full marks every time.
My stuck, bossy thoughts told me
I had to do things to get full marks.

Look back at my story and write about
my stuck, bossy thoughts on the hamster
wheels below.

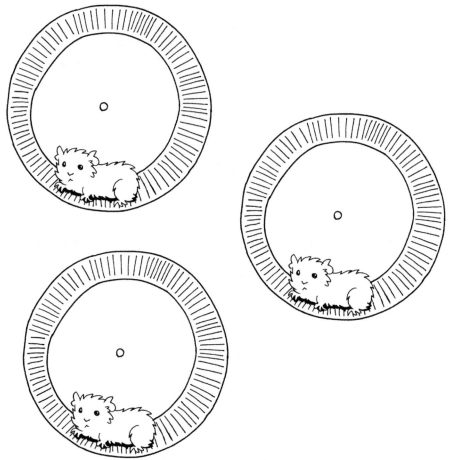

 Stuck and bossy thoughts behave as if they are facts and not just thoughts.

Remember: facts are true and have proof; thoughts are just thoughts, and often have no proof at all.

Did I have any proof that seeing three vans would mean I wouldn't make a mistake?

Or tapping my pencil?

Were these things really linked to doing well in the tests?

These thoughts were just thoughts that had become stuck and bossy.

They tried to make connections where there weren't any.

It's normal to have stuck and bossy thoughts from time to time.

But if the stuck thoughts change your behaviour, they can become a problem.

My stuck thoughts began to affect my behaviour.

Look back at my story and see how they made me miss out on things. Draw your own comic strip below.

My stuck thoughts ...

... made me miss out
on what my friends
were saying

... made me miss
the test questions

... stopped me
from sleeping.

Stuck and bossy thoughts can get stuck on a loop. They can go round and round so fast that they leave no room for anything else.

Let's think of the things that helped me to slow down the wheel.

It can be really hard to ignore stuck thoughts – and trying to ignore them can sometimes make them come back even stronger.

Try to notice your thoughts, especially if they are unhelpful, stuck and bossy ones.

Keep a diary or jotter of some of your thoughts and note if they are helpful or unhelpful. Look out for the ones that are stuck and bossy! When do they happen?

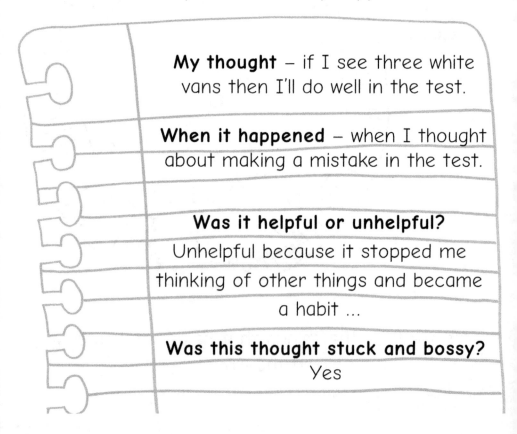

My thought – if I see three white vans then I'll do well in the test.

When it happened – when I thought about making a mistake in the test.

Was it helpful or unhelpful?
Unhelpful because it stopped me thinking of other things and became a habit ...

Was this thought stuck and bossy?
Yes

When you notice a stuck and bossy thought, remember to question it.

Ask yourself ...

... Is this thought a fact and does it have proof ... or is it just a thought?

... Is this thought bossy?

... Is this thought making connections where there aren't any?

... What would I do if a friend was trying to boss me like this?

Sharing the thoughts can slow down the wheel.

Remember to check out your unhelpful, stuck thoughts with someone you trust.

Who can you talk to about your unhelpful thoughts? Draw or write about them below.

When I talked to my friend Ruby, she helped me to recognise that I didn't have to do what the stuck and bossy thought said.

How did Ruby help me to understand about my stuck and bossy thoughts?

Look back at my story and then make your own comic strip below.

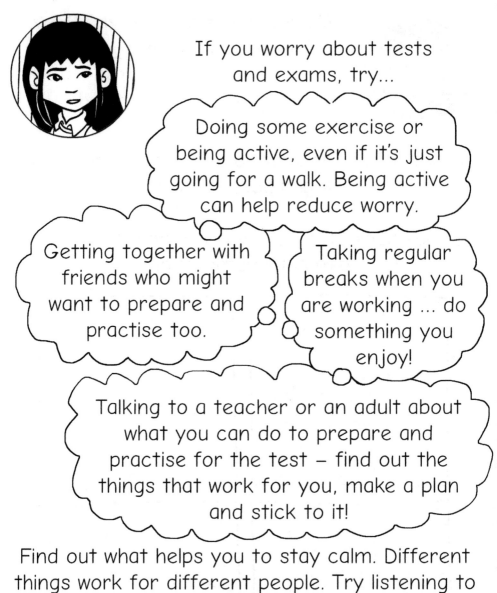

If you worry about tests and exams, try...

Doing some exercise or being active, even if it's just going for a walk. Being active can help reduce worry.

Getting together with friends who might want to prepare and practise too.

Taking regular breaks when you are working ... do something you enjoy!

Talking to a teacher or an adult about what you can do to prepare and practise for the test – find out the things that work for you, make a plan and stick to it!

Find out what helps you to stay calm. Different things work for different people. Try listening to music, reading, drawing or colouring in. Try focusing on your breathing, as you breathe in and out slowly.

Find out as much as you can about what will happen on the day of the test or exam. Get your equipment ready the night before and try to get a good night's rest.

Have a good breakfast – even if you feel a little anxious, try to eat and drink something.

Try to remember that it is normal to feel a little worried about tests – and that a little bit of worry can help us do our very best. Try to notice worry in your body before it takes over and practise your calming activities.

Remind yourself that you can only ever do your best. Always remember that we learn by making mistakes. If you make a mistake, it's not the end of the world ...and the chances are you won't make that exact same mistake again!

If your worry and anxiety grows too big, tell someone you trust straight away.

Summary

• We have lots of different thoughts running through our minds.

• Some thoughts can be helpful and some can be unhelpful.

• Sometimes our thoughts might get stuck and go round and round on a loop in our minds.

• Sometimes these thoughts might be bossy and tell us to do things to stay safe or for good luck. Stuck, bossy thoughts might try to make connections where there aren't any.

• Stuck, bossy thoughts can become a habit and take up all of the space in our minds. Try to notice your stuck, bossy thoughts and remember to question them!

• Check out your stuck thoughts with a person you trust and don't forget to tell someone if an unhelpful thought is bothering you!